Revelation

Date	Lesson	Chapter	Notes
Jan 15	Introduction		
Jan 22	1	Revelation 1	
Jan 29	2	Ephesus	Food for thought
Feb 5	3	Smyrna	
Feb 12	4	Pergamum	
Feb 19	5	Thyatira	
Feb 26	6	Sardis	Food for thought
Mar 5	7	Philadelphia	
Mar 12		**Spring Break**	
Mar 19	8	Laodicea	
Mar 26		**Guest Lecture**	Food for thought
Apr 2		**Guest Lecture**	
Apr 9	9	Revelation 21-22	

Cancellation for KidZone at
www.kidzone.irvingbible.org

DISCOVER TOGETHER BIBLE STUDY SERIES

Psalms: Discovering Authentic Worship
Proverbs: Discovering Ancient Wisdom for a Postmodern World, Volume 1
Proverbs: Discovering Ancient Wisdom for a Postmodern World, Volume 2
Luke: Discovering Healing in Jesus' Words to Women
Ephesians: Discovering Your Identity and Purpose in Christ
1 Peter: Discovering Encouragement in Troubling Times
Revelation: Discovering Life for Today and Eternity

Leader's guides are available at www.discovertogetherseries.com

A Discover Together
BIBLE STUDY

Revelation

Discovering Life for Today and Eternity

Sue Edwards

Kregel
Publications

Revelation: Discovering Life for Today and Eternity
© 2012 by Sue Edwards

Published by Kregel Publications, a division of Kregel, Inc., P.O. Box 2607, Grand Rapids, MI 49501.

ISBN 978-0-8254-4313-8

Printed in the United States of America

12 13 14 15 16 / 5 4 3 2 1

Contents

How to Get the Most Out of a
Discover Together Bible Study   7

Why Study Revelation?   9

LESSON 1   A Preface and a Portrait: Revelation 1   11

LESSON 2   Ephesus: The Church Who Lost Her Love   23

LESSON 3   Smyrna: The Church Who Suffered Well   39

LESSON 4   Pergamum: The Steadfast Church in the
Midst of Evil   51

LESSON 5   Thyatira: The Church Who Tolerated Jezebel   63

LESSON 6   Sardis: The Church Who Looked Good
on the Outside   75

LESSON 7   Philadelphia: The Secure Church on Shaky Ground   87

LESSON 8   Laodicea: The Church Who Nauseated Jesus   99

LESSON 9   Our Eternal Home: Revelation 21–22   111

Works Cited   123

About the Author   125

How to Get the Most Out of a Discover Together Bible Study

Women today need Bible study to keep balanced, focused, and Christ-centered in their busy worlds. The tiered questions in *Revelation: Discovering Life for Today and Eternity* allow you to choose a depth of study that fits your lifestyle, which may even vary from week to week, depending on your schedule.

Just completing the basic questions will require about one and a half hours per lesson, and will provide a basic overview of the text. For busy women, this level offers in-depth Bible study with a minimum time commitment.

"Digging Deeper" questions are for those who want to, and make time to, probe the text even more deeply. Answering these questions may require outside resources such as an atlas, Bible dictionary, or concordance; you may be asked to look up parallel passages for additional insight; or you may be encouraged to investigate the passage using an interlinear Greek-English text or *Vine's Expository Dictionary*. This deeper study will challenge you to learn more about the history, culture, and geography related to the Bible, and to grapple with complex theological issues and differing views. Some with teaching gifts and an interest in advanced academics will enjoy exploring the depths of a passage, and might even find themselves creating outlines and charts and writing essays worthy of seminarians!

This inductive Bible study is designed for both individual and group discovery. You will benefit most if you tackle each week's lesson on your own, and then meet with other women to share insights, struggles, and aha moments. Bible study leaders will find free, downloadable leader's guides for each study, along with general tips for leading small groups, at www.discovertogetherseries.com.

Through short video clips, Sue Edwards shares personal insights to enrich your Bible study experience. You can watch these as you work through each lesson on your own, or your Bible study leader may want your whole study group to view them when you meet together. For ease of individual viewing, a QR code, which you can simply scan with your smartphone, is provided in each lesson. Or you can go to www.discovertogetherseries.com

and easily navigate until you find the corresponding video title. Woman-to-woman, these clips are meant to bless, encourage, and challenge you in your daily walk.

Choose a realistic level of Bible study that fits your schedule. You may want to finish the basic questions first, and then "dig deeper" as time permits. Take time to savor the questions, and don't rush through the application. Watch the videos. Read the sidebars for additional insight to enrich the experience. Note the optional passage to memorize and determine if this discipline would be helpful for you. Do not allow yourself to be intimidated by women who have more time or who are gifted differently.

Make your Bible study—whatever level you choose—top priority. Consider spacing your study throughout the week so you can take time to ponder and meditate on what the Holy Spirit is teaching you. Do not make other appointments during the group Bible study. Ask God to enable you to attend faithfully. Come with an excitement to learn from others and a desire to share yourself and your journey. Give it your best, and God promises to guide you on this adventure that can change your life.

Why Study Revelation?

Crackpots have predicted the end of the world for centuries. Nostradamus, a sixteenth-century Frenchman, prophesied a future doomsday ushered in by cataclysmic events, and his books are still in print. Pseudo-scientists predicted December 21, 2012, as the end, according to an ancient Mayan calendar. Harold Camping missed it three times, insisting that the world would end in 1994, then May 21, 2011, and—once that date passed—October 21 later that same year. In response, atheists created a website, *Eternal Earthbound Pets*, and offered to rescue left-behind cats and dogs for a fee of $135 each.

Nineteen hundred years before Camping's predictions, God told us how the world would *really* end and how to get ready. But he did not tell us when; in fact, he advised us not to speculate.

> But about that day or hour no one knows, not even the angels in heaven, nor the Son, but only the Father. (Matthew 24:36)

Are you ready for the end? In the last book of the Bible, Revelation, the apostle John wrote down the exact words of the risen Christ to help us prepare for our future with him. The book comes alive with color, sound, visions, songs, terror, triumph, warnings, and promises. Jesus even promises to bless us if we read Revelation, and all the more if we heed its instructions.

To me, a study of Revelation seems timely. A few days before the crucifixion, the apostles asked Jesus what signs to expect when his return was imminent. His answer both excites and alarms me.

> Watch out that no one deceives you. For many will come in my name, claiming, "I am the Messiah," and will deceive many. You will hear of wars and rumors of wars, but see to it that you are not alarmed. Such things must happen, but the end is still to come. Nation will rise against nation, and kingdom against kingdom. There will be famines and earthquakes in various places. All these are the beginning of birth pains. (Matthew 24:4–8)

Sure, don't be alarmed by the accelerated pace of natural disasters, conflicts, scarcity, and confusion we observe today. I sense the end is drawing closer. My emotions easily overwhelm me as I consider the future. But a thorough immersion in Revelation has infused me with courage, hope, and excitement. My prayer is that this study will do the same for you.

 Introduction to Studying Revelation (*8:46 minutes*).

I have focused on five special chapters—the first three and the last two—passages that I believe are most pertinent for Christians today. The middle portion of the book describes God's judgments on the earth in its final days. I don't believe Christians will be present during those excruciating days, and I'll explain my reasoning later in this study. I respect other points of view but I find a thorough investigation of these five chapters the most beneficial as we consider how God wants us to prepare for the end.

The first three chapters paint a glorious picture of the resurrected Christ and record his seven letters to first-century churches. These early churches represent the different kinds of churches that have existed through the ages. The letters both commend and point out deficiencies in these churches, providing lessons to help us get ready for our future.

The last two chapters unfold with unspeakable energy, beauty, and promise, as John describes what Jesus shows him: a new Eden, redemption's climax, and our eternal home. Walk with me through these incredible pages, and experience the blessing that God promised to all who read and heed.

A Preface and a Portrait

Revelation 1

Several years ago, my husband and I traveled to Patmos, a tiny Mediterranean island off the coast of Turkey. We waded in the crystal turquoise ocean, walked the rocky white beaches, and climbed the cobblestone streets edged with tiers of white hillside dwellings trimmed in blue. What fun! But the real reason we traveled over six thousand miles was to stand in the cave where Jesus is said to have appeared to John to dictate the book of Revelation. We were overcome as we considered what occurred on this holy ground almost two millennia ago. Here Jesus showed John how the world would end and described the coming of a new heaven and a new earth—finally, a kingdom of justice, truth, and righteousness ruled by the triune God. Our longings fulfilled.

John was known as the apostle Jesus loved; not that he did not love them all, but he held a special affection for John. John was the only apostle who did not run for his life when Jesus was arrested. Instead, he stood beside the women at the foot of the cross. Jesus entrusted the care of his mother to John.

Years later, John was exiled to Patmos for his faith during the reign of the Roman Emperor Domitian. Scholars believe John wrote Revelation in A.D. 95 or 96. Later he was allowed to return to Ephesus, where many believe he died in his bed, the only apostle who was not martyred.

Chapter 1 of Revelation sets the scene and describes the resurrected Christ in all his glory. Savor the richness of John's words. See Jesus in your mind's eye as preparation for the day you will meet him face to face. Get ready!

 God Is BIG (*3:20 minutes*). Scriptural truths can be impressed on our hearts as we observe the world around us. See what we can learn about God the Father and his beloved Son Jesus from a West Highland terrier's encounter with a marauding cardinal.

❋ **Read Revelation 1.**

1. Verse 1 (along with verses 4 and 11) reveals the writers and recipients of Revelation beginning with God the Father and ending with the seven congregations to first hear this book. Fill in the middle blanks with information found in verse 1.

   God the Father → <u>Jesus</u> → <u>his angel</u> → <u>John</u> → Seven Churches

2. According to verse 1, God the Father gave this revelation to the seven churches, and ultimately to all Christians, to show us "what must soon take place." However, almost two thousand years have passed since God birthed the book. In what sense might these revelations take place *soon* for every person who ever lived or will live?

3. Revelation is a circular letter, passed from church to church to be read aloud to the congregation, probably as part of a service. Less than 20 percent of people were literate when this letter initially circulated, necessitating a reader. What is the promise in verse 3? What is the stipulation?

   Blessings do those that read and hear and remember (keep).

4. Do you need a blessing? Consider your concerns over the last week. What weighs most heavily on your heart right now? What do you hope to gain by studying Revelation?

I always need blessings.

5. Verse 4 begins in the typical style of a first–century letter. The author identifies himself, names the recipients, and then greets the hearers with words like "grace and peace to you." Define *grace* and *peace*. How are they different? What would it mean if your life was full of grace and peace?

Grace is being saved even when I don't deserve it.
Peace is calm and quiet within.
Grace is given by God, peace is found within oneself.

For the first twenty-four years of my life I lived without the glorious grace that Jesus bequeaths those who love him. Those years were miserable, hopeless, and unproductive. But when I found Jesus, I found his priceless peace, peace with God and peace with myself and others. I did not experience peace immediately, but over time, as I came to understood the marvelous riches that were mine in Christ. Paul sends grace and peace in his greeting. Don't take these gifts for granted. —Sue

6. John identifies himself as the author in 1:4 but then goes on to include another author who also desires that the recipients experience grace and peace. Who is the other author, and how does John describe him in verses 5, 6, and 8?

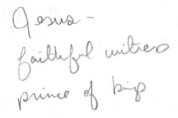

Jesus –
faithful witness
prince of king

SHARED AUTHORSHIP

7. John paints a picture of a throne room in 1:4–8. Who do you think is on the throne?

God

8. Who is in the throne room with him? What do you think they might be doing? Why is their presence important?

The seven spirits

John describes the Spirit as a seven-fold being. In the Bible, seven is the number of perfection or completeness, thus the seven churches represent all churches and the seven spirits represent the Holy Spirit. Scholars refer to Zechariah 4:2 and 10, and Isaiah 11:2 to back up this claim. We also observe references to the seven spirits again in Revelation 3:1; 4:5; and 5:6. "Thus in Revelation the Holy Spirit is sent by the Father and the Son both to be their eyes in this world and to inspire the visions and the prophetic oracles that are the core of the visions" (Osborne, *Revelation*, 37).

9. Verse 7 describes an important event that will usher in the beginning of the end of the world as we know it. What is the event? Now picture the event in your mind; what do you see? Why won't everyone rejoice?

10. The first-century church in Thessalonica had asked Paul questions about the end times, and in a letter to them Paul explained what the Holy Spirit had revealed to him about the event we see described in Revelation 1:7. *Read 1 Thessalonians 4:13–18*. What does Paul say will happen? Why does God reveal these truths to us?

11. How do you feel as you read these prophecies? Excited? Scared? Skeptical? Do these ideas seem far-fetched or difficult for you to believe? Share your honest reactions. If you have overcome any negative feelings, share your thinking with the group.

JOHN'S FIRSTHAND ACCOUNT

The island of Patmos is a little piece of land, eight miles long and five miles wide, in the Aegean Sea about forty miles southwest of Ephesus, where John is believed to have served as the pastor. Today Patmos is a lovely tourist spot, but then it was used by the Romans as a penal colony. John was not under house arrest or in a dungeon. Banishment meant that he had the freedom to roam the island but he was restricted to that locale.

12. John tells us where he was when Jesus appeared to him, why he was there, and even the day of the week. What other details can you glean from Revelation 1:9–10?

"The Lord's Day" most likely refers to the first day of the week, Sunday, when Christians gathered together to celebrate Jesus' resurrection. An early church father, Pliny, wrote that even Roman officials recognized that Christians gathered on a fixed day.

13. See what first alerted John to the fact that Jesus was there (1:10). What might be similar between the sound of a trumpet and the voice of Jesus?

14. What did Jesus tell John to do (1:11)?

The seven specific churches Jesus mentioned were real churches in ancient Asia Minor. Their order is significant because they form the circular route that a letter carrier would have taken, beginning at Ephesus and ending at Laodicea. Each church, as we will see later in our study, had its own particular set of problems, and serves as an example for us even today.

15. When John turned around to locate the voice speaking to him, he saw an amazing vision of the exalted Christ (1:12–16). He used the phrase "like a son of man" to describe what he saw. Centuries earlier, Daniel also experienced a vision of one "like a son of man." *Read Daniel 7:13–14*. What do you learn? What do you think John was saying when he used this term?

Some women see Jesus as a policeman, eager to catch and punish them. Others see him as a cosmic Santa, anxious to spoil them. Some see the portrait that hangs in the church foyer that shows him as pale, meek, and mild—someone who wouldn't hurt a fly. And some think of him like "the force" from *Star Wars*, without much substance. It's hard to entrust your life to these false perceptions. They are all wrong and cause us to look for other gods. But a right view of Jesus will help us love, trust, and worship him with the reverence he alone deserves.

DIGGING DEEPER

This was not the first time John saw the exalted Christ. Read Mark 9:2–4, Luke 9:28–31, or Matthew 17:1–3 to learn about the first time John saw Jesus in all his glory. Study how men and women in the Bible typically responded to seeing God or an angel. Why? What does the divine Person or angel usually say or do?

16. What do you think most people see when they see Jesus in their mind's eye? What do you see? In your opinion, why?

17. Use words, pictures, or symbols to depict what John saw in Revelation 1:12–16:

- His attire

- His head

- His hair

- His eyes

- His feet

- In his right hand (see also verse 20)

- Out of his mouth

- His face

- Objects surrounding him (see also verse 20)

18. How did John react when he saw the exalted Jesus (1:17)? How do you think you will react?

19. What did Jesus do and say to John (1:17–18)? How do you think these words might have impacted John?

DIGGING DEEPER

Paul weighed in on this discussion related to end times, death, and the resurrected Christ. What do you learn from 1 Corinthians 15:50–58 that relates to our study in Revelation?

DIGGING DEEPER

Both God the Father and God the Son call themselves the Alpha and the Omega, the First and the Last (1:8, 17; 21:6; 22:13). What do you think they mean by using this term to describe themselves? Why is this a significant term, especially as we study Revelation?

20. What does it mean to you that the resurrected Jesus holds the keys to life and death?

If you struggle seeing Jesus as he really is, read the classic by J. B. Phillips, *Your God Is Too Small*.

After Jesus appeared to John and comforted him, Jesus dictated the outline of the book to him. We can divide the book into sections using the structure revealed in verse 19:

Write, therefore,

- what you have seen (chapter 1),
- what is now (chapters 2 and 3 from John's perspective), and
- what will take place later (chapters 4–22).

21. Verse 3 ends with a reason to study Revelation: "because the time is near." Do you believe the time is near for Jesus to return and usher in the end? If so, why? If not, why not?

22. Review this lesson. What did you learn that you did not know before? How do you feel as you embark on a study of the end of the world as we know it?

Ephesus

The Church Who Lost Her Love

The first people to learn how the world will end belonged to seven first-century churches in Asia Minor. Jesus explicitly told John to write the message of Revelation on a scroll and send it to these particular churches. As we study Jesus' words to each church, we will see that those churches faced the same kinds of challenges we face today. Some thrived while others limped along. Two of the churches, Smyrna and Philadelphia, received glowing letters of commendation from Jesus. One, Laodicea, earned bad marks all around. The other four heard both praise and rebuke, typical of most churches.

As we study each letter, we will see what Jesus values in a church, and in the individuals who make up congregations. We will learn what pleases him, and be challenged to change. Jesus will hint at incredible rewards that await us when we overcome our tendencies to sin. Most of us will learn something new, as a thorough investigation of Jesus' letters is often neglected. As Jesus dictated each letter to John, he tended to follow a similar pattern, although some elements differ here and there. For example, the letter to the church at Ephesus can be laid out like this:

To:	the church in Ephesus
From:	Jesus (who holds the seven stars and walks among the lampstands)
Praise:	hard work, perseverance, sound doctrine, hatred of false practices
Flaw:	lack of love
Consequence:	possible death of the church
Call:	listen well
Reward:	fruit from the tree of life

Understanding the elements and flow of each letter will help us unlock hidden treasures. Each time we study a new letter, I will lay out the structure for you. My goal is to help simplify the structure, making it easier to see the similarities and differences between the letters. Seeing the

structures should also help you remember what you study. In each letter, after Jesus identifies the recipient, he includes a characteristic about himself, usually from Revelation 1:12–16. For example, in the letter to the Ephesians, Jesus reminds us that he holds the seven stars in his right hand and walks among the seven golden lampstands. In most of the letters, we observe a connection between these characteristics and something related to that particular church. Often the reward will also correspond to something related to the church. Like a puzzle, it is fun and challenging to try to figure out the connections. Occasionally the connection is obvious. At other times, it's more difficult to ascertain. We may not always agree. But looking at the various elements and how they relate can enrich and deepen our study. Let's begin our journey by investigating the first of the seven— the church who lost her love.

 Read Revelation 2:1–7.

More than a quarter of a million people inhabited Ephesus, a center of commerce and one of the most prosperous provinces in the Roman Empire. She was known for her temple to the fertility goddess Artemis, with thousands of priests and priestesses, many of them sacred prostitutes. The temple was four times the size of the Parthenon in Athens, and is one of the seven wonders of the ancient world. Emperor worship also thrived in Ephesus by this time. A temple to the Roman Emperor Domitian had been constructed there.

When John realized that Jesus' first letter would be to the church at Ephesus, his heart probably skipped a beat, because John was believed to have been the bishop of that church for many years. Paul, with the help of Priscilla, Aquila, and Apollos, founded the church some forty years earlier (Acts 19), but John led the congregation before he was exiled to Patmos. The Ephesian church was the most prominent church in Asia Minor, the mother church of all others in the region, and it possibly enjoyed the same kind of reputation that some megachurches enjoy today. But what did Jesus think of the church?

FIRST WORDS

1. Specifically, whom is the letter addressed to and whom is it from (2:1)?

The church of Ephesus
the congregation

From Jesus

The Greek word *angelo* is usually translated "angel," as identified in Revelation 1:20. A guardian angel designated to watch over each church would remind readers of divine forces at work. However, some scholars translate the word as "messenger" and others say this word refers to the human pastor or leader of the church. All these interpretations are possible.

2. What do you think might be the significance of Jesus holding the seven angels (or messengers) in his right hand and walking among the seven lampstands, representing the seven churches? (See Revelation 1:20.)

Jesus holds the congregation of the churches in his hands & can give or withhold life

3. Jesus knows the practices, deeds, and reputation of the church at Ephesus. What does he commend (2:2–3)?

*hard work
patience
intolerance of evil & liars*

4. What challenges do you think a church located in a city like Ephesus would have faced?

*Materialistic
forget the spiritual for the material
love things instead of each other*

Several years ago my husband and I visited the ancient ruins of Ephesus. We wanted to walk the stone streets that first-century Christians walked, to stand in the stadium where our first church leaders preached, and to see what was left of the city with our own eyes. We were not disappointed. The Ephesian ruins may be the best preserved in the world. I particularly remember a long row of outdoor stone toilets where slaves would sit to warm up the seats for their owners. —Sue

LESSON 2   25

5. Jesus praised them for their love of sound doctrine and for discovering false teaching in their midst and exposing it. Have you ever witnessed this process in a church? (No names, please.) If so, what happened?

Does the Doctrine shape God or does it shape you

We must learn to "test" the leaders in our churches and make certain their orthodoxy is sound. We must do so carefully, however, for at the same time there are "heresy hunters" who attack for any doctrinal difference whatever and seem to be interested in power as much as truth. The key is to separate between cardinal doctrines (issues that are clear in Scripture and essential for the Christian faith) and noncardinal issues (points that are not as clear in Scripture and are not essential for remaining a Christian). We must discipline believers on the first . . . but dialogue on the second.
—Grant Osborne
(*Revelation*, 125)

6. What constitutes sound doctrine? What are the essentials of the faith? What truths must a church follow in order to be orthodox?

Following the word of God
Believing in Jesus

7. In contrast, what are some "gray issues" that Christians may disagree
about, while still being considered true to the faith?

Drinking
Dating
Smoking

If there were hundreds of you in your church would it flourish or fail

8. Why was sound doctrine so important for the Ephesian church and
why is it so important for us today?

The apostle John was known as the apostle of love. Tradition says that in Ephesus, where he was the pastor for many years, in his old age he reduced his sermons to one sentence which he would repeat at every church meeting, "Little children, love one another."

9. Despite their emphasis on sound doctrine, service, and perseverance, what caused Jesus to rebuke the Ephesians (Revelation 2:4)? What do you think he meant by his reprimand?

They forgot their first love. Their labour n patience was for material rather than love.

I commend your zeal. But where is your love? For on that your very survival as a church depends. Such a failure is only too possible. It has to be confessed by all Christians who have cast themselves in the role of Mr. Valiant-for-Truth, and forgotten that they are also expected to be Mr. Great-Heart [allusions to characters in John Bunyan's *Pilgrim's Progress*].
—Michael Wilcock
(*Message*, 44)

10. During Jesus' earthly ministry, an expert in the law asked him to define what God most desires from mankind. Jesus answered with Matthew 22:37–40, known as the Great Commandment.

"Love the Lord your God with all your heart and with all your soul and with all your mind." This is the first and greatest commandment. And the second is like it: "Love your neighbor as yourself." All the Law and the Prophets hang on these two commandments.

Consider the two parts of the commandment. How does the first part impact the second part? Circle the key words. Why do you think Jesus values loving God and others over sound doctrine, service, and perseverance?

If you love God & others you will do the right thing

11. Which takes precedence—love of God or love of people? What does Jesus tell us in Matthew 10:37 and 1 Corinthians 7:32–35?

Love of God

We shouldn't love anyone more than we love God.

Unmarried people should love God first; married people should love each other

12. What does it look like to truly love God with all your heart?

To have faith, To obey his commandments, To try to be as much like Him as possible.

To love All others

13. What does it look like to truly love God with all your soul?

To treat others as God would.

Soul (breath) the life of you
Spiritual

Jesus lived his life "interrupted" in the moment

14. What does it look like to truly love God with all your mind?

To continually seek wisdom & knowledge

Some churches die from lack of outreach, lack of planning for the rising generation, or lack of courtesy to visitors; some churches, like the church in Ephesus, may risk simply killing themselves off by how they treat others.
—Craig Keener
(*Revelation*, 113)

15. What does it look like to truly love others?

To treat them as God would.
To put them first

DIGGING DEEPER

Paul wrote his first letter to the church at Corinth because they lacked love and were experiencing multiple problems as a result. Read 1 Corinthians 13. How might this chapter have helped the church at Ephesus?

DIGGING DEEPER

In 1 Corinthians 13:13, Paul wrote, "And now these three remain: faith, hope and love. But the greatest of these is love." In what sense is love greater than faith and hope? When will faith and hope no longer be needed but love still remain?

16. Do you find it more difficult to love God or to love others? Why?

I find it more difficult to love others because they are not perfect like God

17. Why is service without love displeasing to Jesus? How might a lack of love nullify service and sound doctrine?

Without love we have the wrong priorities.
Without love we put things & desires above others

18. What happens in a church when there is sound doctrine without love? Have you ever experienced this? (No names, please.) If so, what resulted?

Some in the church at Ephesus were second and even third generation believers who were fulfilling Christ's prophecy in Matthew 24:12: "the love of many will grow cold" (NET). We are never guaranteed that our children will be as sold-out to Jesus as we are, and the church in any particular region is only one generation away from extinction. Remember to build into the next generation with more than a cold orthodoxy. Love them so that the love of God may be caught and passed on.

19. How do you think the nonbelievers in Ephesus viewed the Ephesian church? What happens to the witness of a church when the congregation lacks love?

non believers probably viewed them as hipocrites.
Witnesses would not feel moved to join the church or even consider what members have to say.

I like your Christ but I do not like your Christians. your Christians do not act like your Christ. Ghandi

20. Jesus exhorted the Ephesians, and any Christian without love, in the first half of Revelation 2:5. What did he tell them to do first? What do you think he meant? How might this have helped them regain their first love?

He tells them to remember where they come from & repeat.

Consider repeat

21. If you have been a believer for some years, recall how you felt when you first came to faith. Have you lost any of the early passion and fervor? If so, why? If not, how have you kept the fire for Jesus kindled?

When I find came to faith I was astounded at the simple truth. I found peace & awe at the marvelous beauty.

I try to remember who I am & where I come from.

22. What does it mean to repent?

To genuinely seek forgiveness

23. Finally, Jesus told them to do the things they did at first. What are some things you did as a new Christian that you no longer do? How might taking up these things again increase your love for God and others?

Study more, pray more, share faith.
These things keep us aware of our love & help us to remember to treat others w love

CONSEQUENCES

24. Jesus said that if the Ephesians did not repent, he would remove their lampstand from its place (Revelation 2:5). What do you think this means? Does the penalty fit the crime or does this seem severe to you? What do you learn by this consequence?

He would take away the promise of Heaven

If I have the gift of prophecy and can fathom all mysteries and all knowledge, and if I have a faith that can move mountains, but do not have love, I am nothing.
—1 Corinthians 13:2

I wonder if it's God's design that we do not know the heresy of the Nicolaitans. If we knew, and their heresy did not apply to us, we might dismiss the warning. But our uncertainty gives the Holy Spirit more flexibility in convicting us of sin, false doctrine, and blind spots in our own lives.   —Sue

Are your ears awake? Listen. Listen to the Wind Words, the Spirit blowing through the churches.
　　　　—Revelation 2:7 MSG

25. Have you ever been part of a church or ministry that closed its doors? If so, what happened? How did you feel? (No names, please.)

No

In Revelation 2:6, Jesus inserted a short commendation that praised the Ephesians for detesting the practices of the Nicolaitans. We don't know who these people were, but assume they were led astray by a false teacher.

THE CALL

26. In every one of the seven letters, Jesus includes the following words:

Whoever has ears, let them hear what the Spirit says to the churches.

- Rephrase this statement in contemporary terms.

Everyone should study & seek to understand Gods word.

- What is significant about the fact that *churches* is plural?

This means all people

- Why do you think Jesus includes the Spirit in this admonition?

So that we will look within

27. In every one of the seven letters, Jesus addresses the part concerning rewards to "the one who is victorious" (2:7). What do you think this means?

Earning everlasting life

Going to Heaven

Overcoming temptation

28. Are all Christians victorious (see 1 John 5:5)? In what sense might they all "win out"? In what sense do they fall short?

No, all Christians are not victorious.

Most follow some commands but also have challenges.

We all forget God sometimes.

 Discipline Your Sin! (*4:59 minutes*). Do you have a few "pet sins" hanging around in your life? Learn how to tame them before they do serious damage.

29. Do Christians who do not gain victory in every area of their life lose their salvation, just their rewards, or both?

Just their rewards

DIGGING DEEPER

How is the great white throne judgment in Revelation 20:11–14 different from the judgment seat of Christ (bema) in 2 Corinthians 5:10?

For a captivating story about the bema seat, read *The Bema: A Story About the Judgment Seat of Christ* by Tim Stevenson.

30. How do Christians overcome the struggles and temptations in life? What has helped you gain victory? In what areas of your life are you still vacillating between victory and defeat?

Remember their love of God
Faith, Prayer, Study
Emotional life, physical temptation

31. Jesus says he will give victors "the right to eat from the tree of life, which is in the paradise of God" (Revelation 2:7). What do the following passages teach you about this tree and its reward? What do you learn about God's redemptive plan throughout history?

Genesis 2:8–9

It is the tree of life
& knowledge

Genesis 2:16

It is ok to eat from every
other tree but the tree of Life

Genesis 3:22–24

Eating from the tree of life made man
understand good & evil as God
does.

Revelation 22:1–3

Do you see the striking imagery in these verses? When our first forefathers sinned, they were denied access to the tree of life, and thus, death entered into the world. But when Jesus returns we will again enjoy the fruit of that tree that sustains eternal life. What a beautiful picture!

32. Why do you think Jesus described himself holding the seven stars and walking among the lampstands as he addressed this particular church? Why do you think he chose to talk about eating from the tree of life as a reward?

Heaven is for real

33. What has most impacted you in Jesus' letter to the church at Ephesus—the church who lost her love? Do you have any new insight? Any new application for how you will live this week?

We should remember the love of God always.

I will try to remember to treat everyone of love.

Smyrna

The Church Who Suffered Well

Why, God?" may be the question people ask God more than any other. When we, or a loved one, are diagnosed with a disease, when children are harmed or disappointed, when people betray us, we ask God "why?" Seldom do we get a definitive answer. Is there any value in suffering?

My pastor's sermon was on suffering the week I was preparing to write this lesson. I'm never surprised at the way God orchestrates lessons for me and I'm hoping to complete this study without a major crisis in my life. None of us welcomes suffering. But my pastor called upon us not to think of suffering as an intrusion but rather as a calling. He asked us to make our suffering holy, meaningful, and redemptive, with Christ as our example.

Jesus wrote his second letter to Smyrna, a group of people enduring severe affliction. He commended them for their present suffering and encouraged them in future trials that would surely come. The structure of the letter looks like this:

To:	the church at Smyrna
From:	Jesus (the First, the Last, the Resurrected One)
Praise:	enduring trials well
Solution:	replace fear with faith
Call:	listen well
Rewards:	the crown of life, protection from the second death

Note that the church at Smyrna was one of only two churches that did not displease Jesus. No flaw is listed. The name *Smyrna* means "myrrh," an aromatic perfume used to embalm the dead and also used as heated oil in prayer vessels. Just as the sweet aroma of myrrh filled the air when the congregation prayed, the response of these brave Christians to their suffering filled the nostrils of God as a sweet aroma.

In tandem with the theme of suffering, Jesus includes resurrection as a

secondary emphasis. Smyrna was a large seaport thirty-five miles north of Ephesus, but unlike Ephesus today, Smyrna continues to be a prosperous city of over 200,000, now Izmir, the second largest city in Turkey.

> Seven hundred years before, old Smyrna has been destroyed, and had lain in ruins for three centuries. The city of John's time was one which had risen from the dead . . . resurrection was to be the experience of its church also. (Wilcock, *Message*, 45)

The immediate picture looked grim for the church at Smyrna, but, just like Jesus, they rose to thrive out of the ashes of persecution and death. We can too. In what other ways might we apply this letter to our lives today?

> This is a letter especially for those who are going through hard times. . . . There are four levels at which persecution can apply in a society like ours where overt persecution seldom occurs: we can identify with the many Christians who are suffering around the world; we can realize that such persecution could happen here in the near future and be ready for it; we can ask ourselves how many compromises we have made in order to avoid any persecution at work or in secular society; and we can endure general trials that draw us away from the world and toward Christ. Any of these can fit this letter. (Osborne, *Revelation*, 136)

 Read Revelation 2:8–11.

FIRST WORDS

1. Why do you think Jesus identified himself as "the First and the Last, who died and came to life again" to the Christians in Smyrna?

2. Do you believe Jesus Christ rose from the dead? If so, what difference has that reality made in the way you live? If not, what are the roadblocks that cause you to doubt this claim?

Like their city, their Lord also "died and came to life," and guarantees a resurrection for them too.
—Michael Wilcock
(*Message*, 45)

PRAISE

3. Jesus begins 2:9 with the words *I know* and then goes on to list the specific challenges facing the church at Smyrna. What difference does it make that Jesus *knows* their struggles and yours? Do you always *feel* that Jesus knows? What can you do when you are in the midst of suffering and don't sense that Jesus knows or cares?

4. Jesus lists three specific struggles the congregation faces at that time: afflictions, poverty, and slander (2:9). The Greek word *afflictions* is singular and is the general word in the New Testament for various kinds of trials and struggles. Obviously, Christians in Asia Minor at this time were in a tight spot! Being a Christian meant suffering economically,

socially, and even, for some, physically. What kinds of sacrifices do Christians today endure for their faith?

5. How do you think you might respond if you were asked to sacrifice a job, social position, or physical comfort for your faith? How can you prepare now for these possibilities?

6. Jesus says the Smyrnaeans are both poor and rich. In what sense is it possible to be both?

7. Jesus saw that these brave men and women were experiencing verbal abuse, specifically slander. People were telling lies behind their backs, lies that damaged their reputations and prospects. Have you ever experienced slander? (No names, please.) If so, how did you feel? What happened? What did you learn?

8. At times, opposition and slander come from within the community of faith. What happened to Paul in Philippians 1:15–26? What was his attitude toward this opposition?

 Slander (*3:19 minutes*). Slander is especially painful when the source is another Christian. What can you learn about God in life's painful experiences?

The enemy is strong. Behind these Jews stands Satan; it is he, not Abraham, who is their spiritual father (John 8:33, 44). But behind Satan stands God, and God is in final control. . . . God's control does not mean that Satan is prevented from inflicting pain and hurt. . . . But what God does guarantee is that though the church may suffer even the death of the body, she will not suffer the death of the soul.

—Michael Wilcock
(*Message*, 46).

9. The root word for Satan's name comes from the Greek word for *accuser* or *slanderer*. How is Satan, the father of lies, behind slander and conflict? What does he hope to accomplish? See John 8:44, 2 Corinthians 11:13–14, and Mark 4:15 for insight.

It is critical not to misinterpret John's comments about the Jews in Smyrna. Some Aryan supremacists have misused this passage to oppress and devalue Jews. John would be horrified. We must all guard against prejudice (see James 2:8–10).

Jesus revealed that he knew where slander against Smyrna originated, from the large and highly visible Jewish population there. This group called themselves Jews, but to Jesus, they were not the children of Abraham as they claimed, because they had not recognized their Messiah (John 8:42–47; 16:1–4). Sadly, early religions opposed the young church more than secular powers. For example, Polycarp was the bishop in Smyrna after John. The Jews denounced Polycarp and the church to the Roman authorities for refusing to worship the emperor. Early historians report that the Jews brought legal action against the Smyrnaean Christians, making their lives miserable, and even helped gather wood to burn Polycarp at the stake. Jesus used harsh language, calling the Jews at that time *the synagogue of Satan*. They were tools in Satan's hands against God's people in the church at Smyrna. However, we must never use these verses to incite anti-Semitism, as some have done. "Always be prepared to give an answer to everyone who asks you to give the reason for the hope that you have. But do this with gentleness and respect" (1 Peter 3:15).

SOLUTIONS

10. Jesus knows our tendencies when we suffer. In Revelation 2:10, what are his first words of comfort? Have you learned to overcome this tendency when you enter into a trial? If so, share with the group what you think and do as you enter into the pain of affliction.

Most scholars believe that the reference to suffering for ten days means that their persecution would only last for a limited time, under the sovereign hand of God.

DIGGING DEEPER

Jesus taught his disciples a similar lesson by taking them through a fearful experience (Luke 8:22–25). How did Jesus create the lesson and what did the disciples learn?

11. Being imprisoned on false charges must be frightening. Who would orchestrate this experience for some Christians in Smyrna (2:10)? What do you think would be the worst part of it for you?

Both faith and fear sail into the harbor of your mind, but only faith should be allowed to anchor.
—Author unknown

12. In addition to overcoming fear, what does Jesus tell them, and us, to do when we find ourselves in overwhelming situations (2:10)?

If your knees knock, kneel on them.
—Sign outside a London church during World War II

Never be afraid to trust an unknown future to a known God.

—Corrie ten Boom

13. Jesus did not ask the Smyrnaeans, or us, to suffer in ways that he himself has not suffered. *Read Hebrews 2:14–18 and 4:14–16.* Why is Jesus an inspiration to us when we face difficult challenges?

14. What did Jesus give up to help us in our weaknesses (Philippians 2:5–11)? How does he advise us to go through tough times?

15. In Romans 8:9–16, Paul explains why it is impossible for us to overcome suffering on our own. What should go on inside believers when they attempt to stand strong in the midst of unjust suffering?

16. Have you experienced the internal strength described in Romans 8:9–16? If so, please help others understand this amazing phenomenon.

DIGGING DEEPER

Paul wrote to the Corinthian church, explaining the suffering he experienced throughout his ministry (2 Corinthians 6:3–10). What kinds of challenges did he and his team face? What helped him through these times without dishonoring the God he loved so much?

REWARDS

17. Jesus speaks about two rewards for Christians who suffer well. What are they (Revelation 2:10–11)?

Like Daniel and his friends, we prepare best for more strenuous future tests by passing the ones we are given in the present. But when we remain faithful in the face of rejection and persecution, Jesus promises us a reward far greater than the power and status our oppressors now enjoy.
—Craig Keener
(*Revelation*, 121)

18. Smyrna was famous for its athletic games where garland wreaths were placed on the heads of victors. Why was a crown a fitting metaphor for Jesus' letter to Smyrna? In what sense does this reward fit the Christians in Smyrna?

19. *Read Revelation 20:11–15.* What is the second death? How do you feel as you read this passage?

FINAL THOUGHTS

20. *Read Revelation 21:6–8.* Look for connections between this text and the letter Jesus wrote to the suffering saints in Smyrna. What similarities do you see?

To live with fear and not be afraid is the final test of maturity.
—Edward Weeks

21. What was Paul's final analysis of his suffering (Romans 8:18)?

22. What do you think is the value of suffering? What lessons have you learned through your challenges and struggles?

23. What have you learned from Jesus' letter to the suffering saints in Smyrna that might help you suffer well in the future?

Pergamum

The Steadfast Church in the Midst of Evil

What voices draw you closer to Jesus? The internet? YouTube? Television programs and advertisements? Films? Video games? Billboards? Occasionally uplifting words come across your screen, a book might inspire you, a friend's e-mail might precipitate a more intimate connection with God—but most of the time, the blaring messages distract you from a rich, full spiritual life. Everything in Pergamum distracted the Christians too. Oh, the pace of life there was slower than ours. Technology did not follow them home. But they lived in a wicked place bent on dirtying them with the mud of the culture, just like we do. Contradictory voices called: *Assimilate. Compromise. Everybody does it.* Another voice countered: *No, don't withdraw from the world or you cannot influence it.* How do we navigate our culture in a manner that pleases Jesus?

British theologian G. B. Caird wrote:

> How narrow is the safe path between the sin of tolerance and the sin of intolerance. (*Revelation*, 41)

Finding our way down that safe path between tolerance and intolerance requires deep insight, wisdom, and discernment. And it's important because there is a ditch on each side of the road. If we err on the side of tolerance, of acclimation, no one can distinguish us from the world. We lose our influence. If we err on the side of intolerance or isolationism, if we huddle together in fear, we extinguish our lamp, and we lose our influence that way too. It's a tight rope, a balancing act, and our witness depends on our getting it right.

Jesus commended the church at Pergamum for getting it right, sort of. Most of them were walking the tightrope admirably. And Jesus praised them for it. But a few in their midst were muddying the water . . . one bad apple . . . a little leaven . . . a problem in some faith communities today. What can we do? A thorough study and discussion of Jesus' letter to Pergamum should keep us out of the ditch.

OPTIONAL

Memorize
1 John 2:15–16

Do not love the world or anything in the world. If anyone loves the world, love for the Father is not in them. For everything in the world—the lust of the flesh, the lust of the eyes, and the pride of life—comes not from the Father but from the world.

The term *world* is not referring to the celestial body or planet known as the earth but instead to the world systems currently dominated by Satan.

The structure of the letter looks like this:

To:	Pergamum
From:	Jesus (who has the sharp, double-edged sword)
Praise:	faithfulness in the midst of a wicked pagan place
Flaw:	tolerance of polluters among you
Solution:	repent and cast them out
Consequence:	otherwise I will
Call:	listen well
Rewards:	hidden manna and a white stone with your new name on it

Pergamum set inland some twenty miles from the seaport of Smyrna. Pergamum was the intellectual center of the region, with a university and library of 200,000 volumes, competing with Athens and Alexandria for academic notoriety. If Ephesus was the New York of Asia Minor, Pergamum was its Washington, DC, for there the Roman imperial power had its seat of government (Wilcock, *Message*, 47). Roman Emperor Augustus built the first temple designed for emperor worship in Pergamum, making the city a forerunner in cultic worship. Other pagan temples dotted the city, one to Zeus, the savior-god, and another to Asclepius, the god of healing, in the form of a serpent. Pergamum was named after its manufacturing industry that produced parchment paper, called pergamena. Evil camped out on every corner of the city. Not an easy place to overcome an addiction or raise a family, but here, Jesus called the Christian church to shine.

His letter to Pergamum should help us thrive in the midst of our wicked world too. So tighten the high wire, grab your balancing poles, and step out onto the rope with me.

 Read Revelation 2:12–17.

FIRST WORDS

1. The exalted Christ identifies himself as having "the words of him who has the sharp, double-edge sword" in Revelation 2:12. For more insight on this sword, look up the following verses. Where is the sword? What is the sword used for? What do you think this sword stands for?

Revelation 1:16 *The sword comes out of his mouth*

Revelation 2:16

To fight against sinners

Revelation 19:11–15, 21

*I think
The sword stands for the
word of God*

The particular kind of sword referred to in 2:12 was a symbol of Roman justice and might, often used in cavalry charges. The Roman in charge of the province resided in Pergamum and the sword symbolized his total sovereignty over all of life there, even the power to execute his enemies with this kind of sword. Jesus may have chosen to describe His words this way to clarify that ultimate power belongs to God and nothing the pagans can do will change that.
—Grant Osborne
(*Revelation*, 140)

2. How do you normally picture Jesus? Do you view him as meek and mild? Holy and majestic?

I view Jesus as a quiet yet forceful, strong yet gentle, force of nature that might appear (God) mild yet can instill devotion w/ his presence

3. Do you struggle to see him carrying and wielding a sharp, double-edged sword? If so, why? What do you think Jesus will actually look like when you see him in the future?

I think the sharp double edged sword is symbolic of his words

We need to be sure we are influencing the world with the kingdom's values, not embracing the world's values where they conflict with those of the kingdom.

—Craig Keener
(*Revelation*, 128)

4. How does Jesus describe Pergamum in 2:13? What do you think he means?

Good people who allow Satan t dwell among them

5. Jesus also knows where you live. How do you think he would describe your locale?

A worldly place

6. What factors in your culture are completely opposed to the doctrine of Christianity? List them. Star those that tend to draw you away from a vibrant healthy faith.

Materialism

Sensualism

Pride

Arrogance

7. When was the last time you felt bombarded by the world and its temptations? How did you respond?

8. Why does Jesus affirm the Christians in Pergamum (2:13)?

   They dwell where Satan dwells
   & continue to do good works.

9. Under pressure, have you ever wanted to renounce your faith in Jesus?
   What kinds of situations might tempt you to be ashamed of the gospel
   or want to leave your faith?

   No

   I can't imagine anything

Look up the following verses and rephrase each in contemporary language. How do these verses help you determine how to be *in* the world but not *of* the world?

· Matthew 5:13–16

· Matthew 22:39

· Matthew 28:19

· Romans 12:1–2

10. Consider "the safe path between the sin of tolerance and the sin of intolerance" (Caird, *Revelation*, 41) as you navigate living in your culture. How do you decide when to be involved enough in the world to understand and influence it, while protecting yourself from contamination?

Live as a example

be tolerant but not indulgent

Live in the world but not of the world.

 Gray Areas (*5:51 minutes*). What should you do when faced with various gray issues in the Christian life? With biblical wisdom and sage advice, Sue concludes, "When in doubt, live love out!"

FLAWS

During Israel's forty-year wanderings in the desert, before they entered the Promised Land, they were tempted to denounce and dishonor God through the influence of surrounding pagan nations. One such incident involved Balaam, an Old Testament Gentile diviner. With the help of Balak, King of Moab, Balaam enticed Israelite men to indulge in sexual immorality with Moabite women. This led to the Israelite men sacrificing to pagan gods, eating the sacrifices, and worshipping these gods. Their actions brought about severe judgment on themselves and on the women who participated, and this resulted in a plague on the Israelites who tolerated their idolatry. "They were the ones who followed Balaam's advice and enticed the Israelites to be unfaithful to the LORD in the Peor incident, so that a plague struck the LORD's people" (Numbers 31:16).

11. Obviously Balaam was not a member of the church in Pergamum. Nevertheless, Jesus insisted that a Balaam-like leader lived and taught among them (Revelation 2:14). What resulted from his influence?

Christians strayed

12. What kinds of enticements (in Pergamum) parallel the Old Testament story mentioned above?

Pagan temples

Eat to every corner

13. What kinds of judgment could the church at Pergamum have expected in light of the account of Balaam and the downfall of the Israelite men?

Plague

DIGGING DEEPER

Today we are not faced with whether or not to eat food sacrificed to idols. However, this issue was important to both Old Testament and New Testament believers. Study 1 Corinthians 8 to learn how Paul instructed that church to deal with this and other gray issues.

14. Sexual immorality is a sin that has plagued mankind since our creation. How serious is this sin where you live? Why do you think it is so pervasive in most cultures? What can be done to help men and women overcome this lurid and prevalent temptation?

It is accepted

We don't know specifics about the teaching of the Nicolaitans (2:15), but assume they were also false teachers, wreaking havoc within the congregation.

15. Again, Jesus has promises for "the one who is victorious." How can you be victorious? For insight see John 16:33, Romans 8:5–6, 1 John 2:15–17, and 1 John 5:1–5.

16. What does Jesus advise us to do in 2:16 in order to be victorious? What does this look like in the life of an individual or a congregation?

Repent

Live riteously where ever you are

17. What is the difference between false teaching and preferential differences? Be sure you are dealing with the former before you confront
anyone as a false teacher.

If you believe false teachers have infiltrated your congregation, what
should you do? First, pray. Then seek a mature and confidential adviser.
Again, be sure that you are addressing legitimate false teaching and not
personal preferences. Be sure that you go to the right people: first the
person involved, then witnesses, and finally leaders, in accordance with
Jesus' instructions in Matthew 18:15–17. Additional resources include *The
Peacemaker* by Ken Sande and *Leading Women Who Wound* by Sue Edwards
and Kelley Mathews.

CONSEQUENCES

18. What did Jesus say he would do if Christians in Pergamum did not
handle the problem of false teachers in their congregation themselves
(Revelation 2:16)? Imagine what that might look like.

Jesus would come to fight
against them

Strike them down w/his double
edge sword

19. Would you prefer that the congregation or Jesus handle the situation? Why?

The congregation

Jesus is fine

TWO REWARDS

20. "Hidden manna" is the first reward for those who are victorious (2:17). Relate Exodus 16:3–4 and John 6:41–51 to this reward. What do you think this might mean?

Peace

Scholars differ over the meanings of *hidden manna* and the *white stone with a new name written on it*. The manna might refer to a special kind of spiritual food as a foretaste of heaven. The white stone is even more difficult to determine. Stones or gems were used as tickets for admission to feasts, and pagans wore amulet stones to protect them from evil. Also, stones were given with names inscribed for initiates into cults of pagan gods. As a result this imagery might not be as foreign to the original readers as it is to us. For us, most likely, the stone may reflect the promise in Isaiah 62:2, "you will be called by a new name that the mouth of the Lord will bestow."

21. The second reward is "a white stone with a new name written on it" (Revelation 2:17). Who do you think writes your new name? How would this make you feel? What name do you think Jesus might give you? See also 22:4 and relate that verse to this reward.

Jesus
special

22. After studying the letter to Pergamum, why do you think Jesus identified himself the way he did in 2:12?

    Knowledge can be uplifting or dangerous.

23. What has most impacted you in Jesus' letter to the church at Pergamum—the steadfast church in the midst of evil? Do you have any new insight? Any new application for how you will live this week?

Thyatira

The Church Who Tolerated Jezebel

The church in Thyatira was the smallest and least significant of the seven churches, but their letter is the longest. The city was located on several trade routes and known for its budding commerce and crafts, particularly its shoe-making, purple dye industry, and bronze metalworks. At the time of the letter, Thyatira was common and relatively obscure, but on the road to economic prosperity.

The city was especially known for its trade guilds, or local unions, and most workers were members because of the economic advantage, but also because these groups were the heart of the social and civic life of the city. If you wanted a good job and an opportunity to get ahead, you joined a guild. No harm in that, but here comes the rub for Christians. Each guild had its own patron pagan god or goddess, led by the chief god of the city, Apollo, the sun god. Guild dinner parties included pagan practices that involved meat sacrificed to these false gods and immoral sexual rituals, all abhorrent to Jesus. Pressure on Christians to join was unrelenting, leaving them between the proverbial rock and a hard place, and leaving the church vulnerable to anyone who might help them rationalize a way out. The "anyone" was a woman.

The structure of the letter looks like this:

To:	Thyatira
From:	Jesus (the Son of God with blazing eyes and bright-polished bronze feet)
Praise:	love, faith, service, perseverance, growth
Flaw:	tolerance of Jezebel
Solution:	reject her
Consequence:	she and her followers will suffer
Instruction:	hold on
Rewards:	reigning with Christ; the Morning Star
Call:	listen well

OPTIONAL

Memorize 1 John 5:10

Whoever believes in the Son of God accepts this testimony. Whoever does not believe God has made him out to be a liar, because they have not believed the testimony God has given about his Son.

These pagan religions were the perfect religion for the sexually indulgent; create gods who were lustful and sexually promiscuous, and then worship the gods that have been created in our own fallen image. It unfortunately re-emerges from time to time, sometimes even within an alleged Christian venue.
—Gordon Fee
(*Revelation*, 39)

※ **Read Revelation 2:18–29.**

1. The exalted Christ identified himself as "the Son of God, whose eyes are like blazing fire and whose feet are like burnished bronze" (Revelation 2:18). Compare these words with John's description of him in Revelation 1:14–15. Why do you think Jesus might have chosen these words to describe himself to this church? Imagine what you might think and how you would feel if you saw his eyes and feet described this way.

Eyes of blazing fire see everything

Brass represents judgement

2. Jesus almost always praises his followers before he reprimands them. What does this tell you about the nature of the Godhead?

He is a fair father, he recognizes the struggle to follow His path

3. What is the lesson for us when we evaluate and then provide feedback for friends, family, or coworkers?

Criticism should be balanced w/praise. Everyone has strengths & weaknesses. Our strengths help us to overcome our weaknesses.

4. What is the lesson for us as we evaluate our own attitudes and actions?

We should be honest yet fair in evaluating our own strengths & weaknesses.

I was raised in a home void of praise. But in the women's Bible study where I came to faith when I was twenty-four, praise flowed freely. I remember the first time our small group leader called me to welcome me to the group. I saved a note from the teacher thanking me for something I said in class. Don't ever forget that your words of encouragement may be life to weary souls. —Sue

5. Jesus praised the Thyatirans for five attitudes and actions. What are they and how do they relate to one another (2:19)?

*Works
Charity
Service
Faith
Patience*

6. In the letter to Pergamum, Jesus focused on the false teaching of a man. But in Thyatira, he focused on the corrupting influence of a woman. What did he call her? What did she call herself?

He called her Jezebel

She called herself

a prophetess

7. Although this woman harmed the church, scholars believe it is possible that another woman may have been influential in birthing the church. To learn about her, see Acts 16:14. What is her name? Describe her.

Lydia

8. From the following verses, draw parallels between the Old Testament Queen Jezebel and the women doing so much damage in the church at Thyatira.

1 Kings 16:29–33

1 Kings 18:4

death / destruction

1 Kings 19:1–2

murder

2 Kings 9:22

idolatry

witchcraft

DIGGING DEEPER

Read 1 Kings 21 to learn more about Ahab and Jezebel. Share with the group pertinent insight that will enrich their understanding of this Old Testament couple.

9. Specifically, what was this woman doing (Revelation 2:20b)?

Seducing Christians to promote & to eat sacrifices & false idols

No matter how strongly Christians feel on various sides of debates on end times teachings, women's ministry, spiritual gifts, and other such matters, we must recognize and publicly affirm that those who sincerely hold different views can be committed Christians, brothers and sisters for whom we should lay down our lives.
—Craig Keener
(*Revelation*, 137)

10. Both men and women have led congregations and ministry groups astray by causing conflict and teaching false doctrine. But men and women sometimes go about causing conflict differently. Have you ever experienced conflict instigated by a woman through her teaching or by other means? (No names, please.) If so, please share what happened and what you learned.

 Navigating Conflict (*5:41 minutes*). Generally speaking, men and women view and navigate conflict differently, but Matthew 18:15–17 applies to us all.

SOLUTIONS

11. What was Jesus' hope for this woman and what was her response (2:21)? What does this tell you about how long she had been causing problems in Thyatira?

Jesus hoped that Jezebel would repent. She refused to repent.

CONSEQUENCES

12. Jesus never enjoys disciplining his followers, but sometimes he needs to get their attention and to curb their unhealthy influence. In 2:22, Jesus said he would "cast her on a bed of suffering." What do you think this means?

Sickness

We have all had human fathers who disciplined us and we respected them for it. How much more should we submit to the Father of spirits and live!
—Hebrews 12:9

13. Can you recall a situation when you think you were "cast on a bed of suffering"? If so, please share what you learned.

The undisciplined is a headache to himself and a heartache to others, and is unprepared to face the stern realities of life.
—Wheaton College Bulletin

DIGGING DEEPER

Physical illness is caused by a variety of reasons, but one of the reasons revealed in James 5:13–20 is sin. Read and dissect this passage. What do you learn? Relate this text to Jesus' discipline to help Jezebel in Thyatira.

14. How will the exalted Christ discipline those who followed this woman into sin (2:22b–23a)? How do you feel as you hear the consequences of their sin? What does this tell you about God?

They will have great tribulation

Don't miss the sudden change in personal pronouns in 2:22 and 23. In verse 22, Jesus says "unless *they* repent of *her* ways" warning the congregation at Thyatira. But in verse 23, Jesus speaks to all the churches and says, "I will repay each of *you* according to *your* deeds." The point is that these letters are not just for that time and place, but for all time and for all his followers throughout the ages. Our actions and heart attitudes today will make a difference in our future eternal lives. What a great incentive to live for Jesus!

15. How do you feel toward God as you study the discipline inflicted upon Jezebel and her followers?

Most scholars think the term *children* in 2:23 refers to Jezebel's spiritual rather than biological children.

DIGGING DEEPER

Some people in the Corinthian church fell under God's judgment because of their irreverent and unloving attitudes and actions regarding the Lord's Supper. Read 1 Corinthians 11:27–33. According to verse 30, what was happening to some of their members? What do you think this means?

Beware of anyone who tells you they possess "deep secrets" about God that only certain people are privileged to know. Very likely these people will promote their ideas as sourced in God; however, Jesus gives us the real source of these "deep secrets" in verse 24. Be discerning, dear sisters.

16. Jesus' discipline had several purposes. First it was designed to encourage Jezebel and her followers to repent. Second it was designed to protect those in the church who might come under her influence. What is a third purpose, mentioned in 2:23b?

Everyone will receive blessing or tribulations according to their works.

In 2:23, the exalted Christ says that he will repay believers according to their deeds. This will occur at the bema seat of Christ, the believer's judgment, and will result in rewards and possibly some disappointment. However, Christians do not lose their salvation, which is eternally secure when they come to faith and their names are written in his book of life (1 John 5:10–13; Revelation 20:15).

INSTRUCTIONS TO THE FAITHFUL

17. Jesus commends the faithful for standing firm in the midst of this little church. If believers find themselves in an unhealthy church today, they usually have the option of finding another church. However, the believers in Thyatira probably did not have that choice. Have you ever found yourself wanting to leave an unhealthy church? (No names, please.) What tensions did you face? When do you think it is wise to leave and when is it wise to stay?

18. What did Jesus tell these faithful believers to do (Revelation 2:25)? What do you think he meant?

He told them to hold on.
They would be rewarded of
their faith & strength

REWARDS

Did you know that if you are a faithful follower of Christ you will participate with Christ in the final judgment on the nations? That is the implication in verses 26–27. This passage echoes Psalm 2:4–9, where the Father endows the Son with authority to judge the nations at the end of this earth's history. Justice will prevail and you can be part of it!

19. To those who remain faithful, incredible privileges and rewards await. What is the reward mentioned in 2:26–27?

    Power

20. In Revelation 20:4–6, John describes Christ's thousand-year kingdom and believers' reign with him. What interesting insight can you glean?

21. Where else will Christ's servants reign (21:1; 22:3–5)?

    Heaven & earth

22. What additional reward does the exalted Christ mention (2:28)? See Revelation 22:16 for more explanation. Any ideas about what this means?

Right now, due to the way our solar system is constructed, we cannot see stars in the morning. Consider the implications that Christ will be the bright Morning Star.

FINAL THOUGHTS

23. What has most impacted you in Jesus' letter to the church at Thyatira— the church who tolerated Jezebel? Do you have any new insight? Any new application for how you will live this week?

DIGGING DEEPER

As a review, compare and contrast the letter to the church at Pergamum with the letter to the church at Thyatira. Now relate what you know about these two letters with the first two letters we studied. Consider making a chart to record your findings about these four letters and the next three letters we will study.

Sardis

The Church Who Looked Good on the Outside

Grand and sophisticated, Sardis had a fine reputation, even though most of its splendor lay in the past. We can trace its rich history back to almost 1200 B.C. This city was the first to mint gold and silver coins. It was a respected military stronghold because of its location. Surrounded by sheer cliffs on three sides, Sardis was thought to be virtually impregnable. An outright attack never succeeded, but twice in its history, a soldier climbed the precipice, crawled through a crevice in the rock hill, and snuck in to open the city gate undetected. Sardis fell quickly both times. Twice the city was caught totally off guard. These victories so astounded the Roman Empire that *capturing Sardis* became a saying for achieving the impossible.

In A.D. 17, several decades before the letter, a devastating earthquake destroyed the city but Rome rebuilt it soon after. Pliny the Elder, a Roman writer and magistrate, called the quake the worst disaster in human memory up to that time.

> A huge temple to the fertility goddess Artemis was started there but never finished. The people of Sardis had a special interest in death and immortality, and much of their religious life was nature worship focusing on the fertility cycle and bringing life out of death. A sacred hot springs two miles from the city seems to have been connected with the god of the underworld and these same themes. (Osborne, *Revelation*, 172)

Hints of external or internal pressures or persecution are missing from the letter. In some areas of Asia Minor, Jewish communities were tolerated. Possibly the Christians in Sardis rode the coattails of the large Jewish community there, providing peaceful relationships with other religious groups, but also possibly fostering accommodation to the surrounding culture.

Sardis slowly lost its influence and was conquered by Arabs in A.D. 716. Today only the small village of Sart remains among the ruins of Sardis.

These seemingly random facts about Sardis prepare us for our study

OPTIONAL

Memorize
1 John 5:11–12

And this is the testimony:
God has given us eternal life,
and this life is in his Son.
Whoever has the Son has
life; whoever does not have
the Son of God does not
have life.

of Jesus' letter to the church there. Because in many ways, the church had taken on the personality of the city. And Jesus used its history and present circumstances to teach the church spiritual lessons that would make the difference between life and death.

The structure of the letter looks like this:

To:	Sardis
From:	Jesus (who holds the seven spirits of God and the seven stars)
Flaws:	you are on death's door, fake, clueless, and incomplete
Solutions:	wake up!
Consequence:	Jesus will show up unexpectedly and take care of the problem
Praise:	a few of you are clean
Reward:	life dressed in white
Call:	listen well

 Read Revelation 3:1–6.

FIRST WORDS

1. The exalted Christ paints a picture of himself holding the seven-fold Spirit in one hand and seven stars (representing guardian angels or pastors of the churches) in the other (Revelation 3:1). What do you think he might be communicating in this description? If nothing comes to mind, you may want to come back to this question after you have studied the letter.

 Faith, Hope, and Love (*3:19 minutes*). "And now these three remain: faith, hope and love. But the greatest of these is love" (1 Corinthians 13:13). The book of Revelation holds a clue as to why!

2. In the previous letters we studied, what kinds of words did Jesus use after he described himself? See the structures of those letters. Why do you think this structure may be different?

3. What is the condemnation in 3:1? Write these words in contemporary terms.

Complacent, self-deceived, coasting. A perfect picture of inoffensive Christianity, this church is, for the most part, stone-cold dead. Jesus' letter warns us to look in the mirror and be honest about what we see, and then ask our tender and loving Lord to help us do business with anything that hinders our spiritual growth. Praise God that he is full of grace and for us. Nevertheless we are called to wake up and evaluate our lives periodically. Sobering.

4. God called David a man after his own heart. In Psalm 26, David describes a blameless life before the Lord. According to Psalm 26:4, what is one important aspect of godly character?

5. First Timothy is a New Testament letter Paul wrote to Timothy, his son in the faith. In that letter, Paul explained what would occur during the final years before Christ returns. What kinds of people will lead the church astray in the future according to 1 Timothy 4:1–2? What does this tell you about people who are not who they seem to be?

6. Jesus spoke about this flaw in the Sermon on the Mount. His message began with this main thought: "Be careful not to practice your righteousness in front of others to be seen by them. If you do, you will have no reward from your Father in heaven" (Matthew 6:1). As he continued his message, what specific areas of the Christian life did he address and, in a nutshell, what did he say?

Matthew 6:2–4

Matthew 6:5–8

Matthew 6:16–18

7. What do you think are the underlying causes of hypocrisy, especially related to spirituality? See also Matthew 23:5.

Double-mindedness is a common disease that leaves its victims paralyzed by doubt. How much better to be single-minded! No mumbo-jumbo. No religious phony-baloney. No say-one-thing-but-mean-something-else jive. No Pharisaic hypocrisy where words come cheap and externals are sickeningly pious. The single-minded are short on creeds and long on deeds. They care . . . really care. They are humble . . . really humble. They love . . . genuinely love. They have character . . . authentic character.
—Author unknown
(Swindoll, *Tale*, 287)

8. Jesus rebuked the Pharisees and teachers of the law for valuing their own rituals and traditions above the Word of God (Matthew 15:1–20). Briefly read through this passage. Can you think of specific rituals and traditions that churches today place above God's Word? Give some examples. (No names, please.)

9. Hypocrisy, having a reputation of being one way but actually being another, may have been the sin Jesus hated most. What word pictures did he paint of pretenders? What do you think he was saying through each picture?

Matthew 23:23–24

Matthew 23:25–26

Matthew 23:27–28

Matthew 23:33

Matthew 23:37–38

10. Jesus warned his disciples not to be hypocrites in Luke 12:1–3. Why? When do you think this will occur?

11. How does the desire to keep secrets about who we really are lead to hypocrisy in our lives and in our church communities?

12. What things are most difficult for you to reveal to others? Do you know why you prefer to keep these things hidden?

DIGGING DEEPER

The desire to *fit in* and *look good to others* is typical. Study the account of Peter and Paul in Galatians 2:11–21 and report what you learn about hypocrisy and honesty.

DIGGING DEEPER

Ananias and Sapphira were a Christian couple in the first church in Jerusalem. Study Acts 5:1–11 to learn how they exhibited a hypocritical spirit and how God responded.

13. After studying Jesus' words and actions toward hypocrites, why do you think Jesus was so strong in his rebuke of the church at Sardis? How important is it that individuals and churches address the issue of hypocrisy? Why?

Actors are the only honest hypocrites.
—Author unknown

14. Have you ever been part of a congregation or ministry that looked good on the outside but was *dead* on the inside? (No names, please.) If so, share how you felt and what you learned.

SOLUTIONS

15. Jesus counsels the church to help them begin to heal in Revelation 3:2–3a. List what he tells them to do.

16. Can you think of specific ways an almost dead church could "strengthen what remains"?

17. Have you ever witnessed Christians whose deeds were not complete? What causes this situation? What impact does this have on them and on the congregation?

18. Do you ever struggle to complete what you start? If so, how does this flaw impact your life?

CONSEQUENCES

19. What could happen if the Sardians ignored Jesus' counsel (3:3b)? Any idea why Jesus chose these words to warn them?

20. Have you ever been robbed or accosted? If so, were you surprised? How did you feel? Were there any long-term consequences, and if so, what were they?

21. John paints a more explicit picture of Jesus' warning in Revelation 16:15. What is the picture? What is the consequence? What do you think these words would mean to the Sardians? What is the lesson for us?

PRAISE AND REWARDS

22. Jesus points out that in the midst of this church of hypocrites live a few open, honest Christians attempting to walk faithfully with Jesus. How does Jesus say he will reward them (3:4–5)?

23. John describes the wedding banquet of the Lamb in Revelation 19:6–9. What are the guests wearing? Who provides their garments? How does one become clothed that way (1 John 5:5)?

FINAL THOUGHTS

24. Reread the introduction to this lesson explaining the background of Sardis. In what ways does Jesus' letter to Sardis reflect what happened in the past and was now going on in the city? Can you surmise whether or not the church at Sardis heeded Jesus advice?

If you skipped the first question in this lesson, go back and answer it now.

Asia Minor had a practice similar to ours. They bid on bringing important events to their cities much like we do the Olympics. Sardis thought they could outbid other cities and bring the imperial temple to their town because of their past accomplishments. But they lost the bid to Smyrna, whose appeal was more current. The lesson for us: don't look back. Don't think that you can retire from Christian service because you have "paid your dues." Jesus still needs your gifts, voice, and participation. There is no such thing as retirement for a Christian!

25. What has most impacted you in Jesus' letter to Sardis—the church who looked good on the outside but was rotten on the inside? Do you have any new insight? Any new application for how you will live this week?

Philadelphia

The Secure Church on Shaky Ground

The earthquake aroused me out of a sound sleep. My husband and I were visiting my daughter and her family in Anchorage, Alaska, where I experienced my first earthquake since childhood. In the morning, my daughter informed me that it was just a tiny tremor, no concern, and a common occurrence. The experience reminded me of an afternoon when my parents and I lived on the Aegean island of Rhodes, Greece. I was eleven years old and my father was stationed on the Coast Guard Cutter *USS Courier*, a ship that broadcast behind the Iron Curtain. That earthquake shook the house enough to swing the lights and knock a glass off the counter. Again, small, and no real damage, except to my psyche. Several years ago, when our seventy-ninth-floor San Francisco hotel room swayed in the howling wind, I couldn't wait to return to Texas, where the earth stands still. I like solid footing and secure foundations, something our spiritual ancestors from Philadelphia knew little about.

Philadelphia, located thirty miles southeast of Sardis, was built near an active volcano and on a fault line. While the large plain of lava deposit was perfect for vineyards, the earthquakes made it difficult to live there. Earthquakes completely destroyed the city several times. The same earthquake that leveled Sardis in A.D. 17 also destroyed Philadelphia, but since Philadelphia was nearer the epicenter, she continued to suffer lingering aftershocks. The city walls were continually cracked, people lived in insecure buildings, and many made their homes outside the city, on farms where the ground beneath them shook less.

Despite the challenges, people continued to live in Philadelphia. The city lay on the major postal road to Rome, making her ideal for commerce, and, of course, she was agriculturally prosperous, particularly known for her wine. Her patron deity appropriately was Dionysus, god of wine. Less than two hundred years earlier, two brothers—Eumenes II, king of Pergamum, and his younger sibling Attalus Philadelphus—founded the city, which became known as the city of brotherly love.

In this unstable atmosphere sat a small Christian church, a congregation that pleased Jesus so much that he wrote her a letter containing only

OPTIONAL

Memorize
1 John 5:13
I write these things to you who believe in the name of the Son of God so that you may know that you have eternal life.

87

commendation and encouragement. If the ground under your life seems less than firm, or if you find yourself serving in a small place or attending a small church, you should find Jesus' letter to Philadelphia uplifting and helpful.

The structure of the letter looks like this:

To:	Philadelphia
From:	Jesus (the holy and true One who opens doors for you)
Praise:	you are small but faithful in an unsteady place
Rewards:	your adversaries will honor you; I will shield you from tribulation; you will enjoy stability in my kingdom
Exhortation:	persevere
Call:	listen well

 Read Revelation 3:7–13.

FIRST WORDS

1. In this letter, Jesus describes himself with two adjectives. What are they and why do you think the Philadelphians needed to hear that Jesus possessed these two particular characteristics? If you are unsure, come back to this question after you study the letter.

2. Jesus also describes himself as holding something. What is it? How does Jesus use this object (Revelation 3:7)?

The phrase "key to the house of David" is found in an Old Testament account. This story takes place before the Assyrians carry off the Jews into exile, a judgment from God for their disobedience. In these verses the Lord demands that Shebna, a high court official in charge of Hezekiah's palace, be replaced by Eliakim, a less important palace official but a godly man.

3. *Read Isaiah 22:20–24.* Answer the following questions.

- How would Eliakim be dressed? What resources will be given to him (22:20–22)?

- How will the people of the nation perceive Eliakim (22:23)?

- How might this story have encouraged the Philadelphians and continue to encourage all Christians who encounter unsettling circumstances?

- Can you think of any other ways this story might inspire the Christians in Philadelphia?

4. The exalted Christ now holds the key of David, and what he shuts no one can open, but what he opens, no one can shut. That key opens a door for Christians (Revelation 3:8). Jesus is not clear where the door leads, and scholars disagree. What does an open door symbolize for you?

5. What doors has Jesus opened for you? (Consider salvation, service and ministry opportunities, strength in difficult circumstances, relational healing, etc.)

6. How do you feel knowing that if Jesus opens a door, no one can shut it? Why do you think Jesus includes this point?

7. What doors would you like Jesus to open for you in the future?

8. In addition to enduring frequent aftershocks and earthquakes, Philadelphians were persecuted by the Jewish community. Like Smyrna, Jesus calls them *the synagogue of Satan*, because they believed they were God's chosen people but denied his Messiah, Jesus. These Jews probably excommunicated Christians and closed the door of their synagogue to them, which was typical throughout the ancient Roman world at this time. Jesus was about to give the Philadelphia believers some insight into this situation. What makes a person a "true Jew" (Romans 2:28–29)?

It's critical not to misinterpret John's comments when he refers to the Jewish synagogues as the *synagogues of Satan*. Some Aryan supremacists have misused this passage to oppress and devalue Jews. John would be horrified. We must all guard against prejudice (see James 2:8–10).

9. Have you ever been shut out? How did you feel? What effect do you think Jesus' words in Revelation 3:9 might have had on the Philadelphians?

PRAISE AND REWARDS

10. Write out 3:10, in the space provided. Then answer the questions below.

- What do the words *I will keep you from* mean?

- Jesus speaks of a time of trial. What is the scope of the trial?

- What is the purpose of the trial?

11. The church in Thessalonica asked Paul to explain about that "hour of trial that is going to come on the whole world" and when that time, the day of the Lord, would occur. He answered them in 1 Thessalonians 5:1–10 (provided below in NET version, with emphasis added). Read the text carefully and answer the questions below.

Now on the topic of times and seasons, brothers and sisters, you have no need for anything to be written to you. For you know quite well that the day of the Lord will come in the same way as a thief in the night. Now when they are saying, "There is peace and security," then sudden destruction comes on them, like labor pains on a pregnant woman, and they will surely not escape. But you, brothers and sisters, are not in the darkness for the day to overtake you like a thief would. For you all are sons of the light and sons of the day. We are not of the night nor of the darkness. So then we must not sleep as the rest, but must stay alert and sober. For those who sleep, sleep at night and those who get drunk are drunk at night. But since we are of the day, we must stay sober by putting on the breastplate of faith and love and as a helmet our hope for salvation. *For God did not destine us for wrath* but for gaining salvation through our Lord Jesus Christ. He died for us so that whether we are alert or asleep we will come to life together with him. Therefore encourage one another and build up each other, just as you are in fact doing.

a. Circle the pronouns that refer to nonbelievers (they, them).
b. Underline the pronouns that relate to Christians (you, we, us).

c. What different images and words does Paul use to compare believers and nonbelievers?

d. Will this hour of trial be expected? What will nonbelievers be doing and saying when it arrives?

e. What do you think it means that "God did not destine us for wrath but for gaining salvation through our Lord Jesus Christ"?

f. What is the ultimate purpose for passages like this in the Bible? How might these kinds of words encourage the Thessalonians, the Philadelphians, and us today?

Pretribulation scholars use passages like Revelation 3:10 and 1 Thessalonians 5:9 to support their view that Christians will not be present at the events presented in Revelation 6–18, also known as the Great Tribulation, a seven-year period of time when God pours out his wrath upon the earth. However, other godly scholars hold different ideas on end-time events. Whatever your view, discuss the related questions with grace, kindness, and respect, realizing that these are not issues that should divide brothers and sisters in the family of God.

12. The exalted Christ offers another reward to the saints in Philadelphia in Revelation 3:12. What is it? What picture do you see in your mind's eye?

13. What problem arises when you read 21:22?

14. What is the purpose of a pillar in a temple? In light of the insecure place where they lived, any ideas why Jesus called the Philadelphians a pillar in his temple?

Historical evidence points to the likelihood that Christians in Philadelphia were expelled from the Jewish synagogues. How painful an experience . . . but how comforting. Jesus not only pictured them welcomed into God's temple, but also a constituent part of it.

15. The exalted Christ wrote three different names on each pillar. What were they, and what do you think is the significance of each?

16. What do you think is the significance of the fact that they will never need to leave the temple?

 Envisioning the End (*2:38 minutes*). Envisioning the end of the world can be unsettling and frightening, but God can sooth your fears and help you welcome his eternal plan.

FINAL THOUGHTS

17. Do you sometimes feel like you are living in a shaky place without stability and security? If so, how has this lesson ministered to you?

18 What has most impacted you in Jesus' letter to Philadelphia—the secure church on shaky ground? Do you have any new insight? Any application for how you will live this week?

Laodicea

The Church Who Nauseated Jesus

A few nights ago I awakened to an awful sound. In the dark I turned my head to see the shadow of my cat heaving between our pillows. I jumped up, flipped on the light, and scooped him off the bed just before he brought up whatever his body had determined did not belong in his stomach. I've cleaned up vomit from my husband, my children, grandchildren, cats, and dogs—scenes I prefer not to describe or even think about. But Jesus chose this picture to communicate the way the Laodiceans made him feel—nauseated, sick to his stomach—a warning to us all. They were not beyond hope, but close.

Laodicea was the wealthiest of the cities we have studied—renowned for its premier banking system, the Swiss banks of the ancient world. The city was high fashion, touting the finest quality black wool in the world. It was also high tech for the times. A prestigious medical school made it the place people came for advanced treatments. A famous eye doctor developed a compound, a powder made into a salve, for curing eye diseases. As a result, Laodiceans had a rather high opinion of themselves.

One drawback to living in Laodicea was its lack of water. It had to pipe in water from a nearby hot springs but by the time the water reached them it had cooled down enough to be tepid, insipid, and stale. In addition, the water was full of sediment. Excavation of the water pipes revealed thick lime deposits, suggesting a nasty contamination that made the water foul to smell and drink.

The exalted Christ crafted a letter tailor-made for the church at Laodicea, but its lessons apply to the other six churches, to churches of all time, and to us as individuals. Find out what makes Jesus want to throw up.

The structure of the letter looks like this:

To: Laodicea
From: Jesus (the Amen, the faithful and true
           witness, ruler of God's creation)

OPTIONAL

Memorize Revelation 2:7a, 11a, 17a, 29; 3:6, 13, 22
Whoever has ears, let them hear what the Spirit says to the churches.

OPTIONAL

Review 1 John 5:10–13
Whoever believes in the Son of God accepts this testimony. Whoever does not believe God has made him out to be a liar, because they have not believed the testimony God has given about his Son. And this is the testimony: God has given us eternal life, and this life is in his Son. Whoever has the Son has life; whoever does not have the Son of God does not have life. I write these things to you who believe in the name of the Son of God so that you may know that you have eternal life.

Like city, like church. How fascinating that almost every part of the letter relates to what's going on in the city. Consider ways in which your church is affected by your surrounding community.

Flaws:	you are lukewarm, self-deceived, wretched, pitiful, poor, blind, and naked
Solutions:	buy from me real gold, white clothes, salve to open your eyes; invite me in for rich fellowship
Reward:	reign with me
Call:	listen well

 Read Revelation 3:14–22.

FIRST WORDS

Jesus used the term *the Amen* 13 times in *Mark*, 31 times in *Matthew*, 6 in *Luke*, and 25 in *John* to emphasize a particularly sobering truth.

1. The exalted Christ first describes himself to the Laodiceans as the *Amen*. We often use this word to sign off our prayers, but what does this term mean? Read 2 Corinthians 1:20 and Jeremiah 28:6 for insight.

   Hebrew meaning True

The only good thing in Laodicea is the church's thoroughly good opinion of herself—and that is false.
—Michael Wilcock
(*Message*, 57)

2. What other words does Jesus use to describe himself in the opening of the letter (Revelation 3:14)? Why do you think the Laodiceans need to know these attributes? Why do we? If you are unsure, wait to answer this question until after you have studied the letter.

   The faithful & true witness
   The beginning of Gods creation

3. What is the primary reason Jesus rebuked this church (3:15)? What does this mean? Why would these words be particularly meaningful to the Laodiceans?

Neither hot nor cold, lukewarm

In our culture where children are given awards just for participating and harsh words are viewed as unhealthy (and sometimes for good reason), a harsh rebuke seems unwelcome. But remember that Jesus wants to shake us from our complacency for our great benefit. He died for us and offers us new life here and forever. So take his words to heart and apply them where needed. He speaks for our good and not to harm us.

4. Why do you think Jesus said he would prefer they be cold rather than lukewarm?

They have a position, when you reach bottom you are motivated to change

5. What was Jesus' response to their spiritual state (3:16)?

Rejection

6. Describe a Christian who is lukewarm. (No names, please.) What attitudes and actions are typical?

Someone who doesn't know who you are ...

The only cure for lukewarmness is the re-admission of the excluded Christ.
—G. Campbell Morgan

7. Do you know anyone that you would characterize as spiritually lukewarm? Have you ever been part of a church or ministry that fits this description? If so, why have you come to this conclusion? (No names, please.)

8. Are you *sold-out* to Jesus or do you consider this quality extreme or radical? Discuss.

It can be too extreme or unreasonable

9. Jesus gives us a primary reason Christians can become lukewarm in Revelation 3:17a. What is it and why is it so dangerous in a believer's life?

They forget where their riches come from. And b/c materially you are prosperous you should also consider intellectual/spiritual riches.

In *Letters to the Seven Churches*, Colin Hemer explains that the entire region was rich, and Laodicea was often chosen as the major example of this wealth. Coins from there depict cornucopias, a symbol of wealth and affluence. A man named Hiero bequeathed two thousand talents (several million dollars in today's terms) to the city, and the Zenonid family was so wealthy and powerful that several of their members achieved the status of royalty under the Romans. In A.D. 60 a devastating earthquake leveled the city, but they rebuilt it back better than before, without help offered by Rome (pp. 191–95).

10. Are you wealthy? If so, in what way? How do you measure abundance?

I feel that I am wealthy spiritually.

11. Is it wrong to be materially rich? When can it become a problem? What was God's counsel in Proverbs 30:7–9?

No. When our materials become what we worship

DIGGING DEEPER

Jesus told a parable about a shrewd manager who invested his money wisely. What else can you learn about material wealth from Luke 16:1–15?

The two cities that no longer exist housed the two churches most severely rebuked, Sardis and Laodicea. And the two cities that held out longest before the Turkish conquest are the two churches most highly praised, Smyrna and Philadelphia.

12. Jesus links the Laodiceans' pride, wealth, and smug self-satisfaction with five negative qualities in Revelation 3:17. List them. Are you surprised Jesus would use such strong words? What does this tell you?

wretched

pitiable

poor

blind

naked

It is upsetting to Jesus.

SOLUTIONS

13. Jesus counseled these beloved believers by asking them to *buy* some things (3:18). Why do you think he used this terminology with the Laodiceans? Would this language be appropriate for many Christians you know? For you?

It is language that materialistic people would understand.

Everything is provided by Him.

Refinement
Holiness Wisdom

14. The first thing Jesus wanted them to buy from him is "gold refined in the fire," so they can become rich. Similar imagery is found in other books of the Bible. Study the following passages. What does this precious metal represent? How will they experience true wealth?

Psalm 66:10

Refinement

Isaiah 1:25

Zechariah 13:9

1 Peter 1:3–7

15. Has God *refined* you through particular experiences that enriched your life? If so, please share.

16. Second, Jesus wanted them to buy "white clothes to wear" (Revelation 3:18), so they can cover their shameful nakedness. Why would this request be particularly meaningful in Laodicea?

Purity

Jesus is not saying that nakedness within appropriate intimacy boundaries is shameful, but in the Old Testament, public nakedness was a symbol of shame and judgment (for example, Ezekiel 16:35–39).

17. What does white symbolize to you? What do the following verses tell you about fashion in heaven? Why do you think Jesus asked them to dress in white?

Purity

Revelation 4:4

Revelation 7:9

Revelation 19:14

18. The third item Jesus wanted them to buy is eye salve to alleviate their blindness. Why would this request be particularly meaningful in Laodicea?

Wisdom

19. Were the Laodiceans aware of their blindness (3:17)? What did Jesus want them to see?

No, He wanted them to recognize to repent & give their heart to Him.

20. How important is self-awareness in the Christian life? Are you self-aware? Why or why not?

Know strengths & weaknesses
Know your gifts to better serve
Him.

21. The exalted Christ declares his love for the Laodiceans and all who disappoint him (3:19). In what terms does he express his love? How do you feel about this?

He provides structure & discipline

The Greek root word for "be earnest" in Revelation 3:19 relates to the idea of acting with much zeal. The idea here is not just to repent but to do so whole-heartedly.

22. What was Jesus' answer to their spiritual poverty and blindness (3:20)? Draw the scene or picture it in your mind. Where is Jesus? Where is the lock on the door? What is he asking? How would this kind of fellowship help us overcome lukewarm tendencies?

Although the invitation to dine with Christ is open to the whole Christian community, Jesus phrases it to us as individuals. The strength of the entire fellowship is determined by our personal commitments to love Jesus and live for him only. Will you take your place at his table?

 An Invitation (*3:03 minutes*). Revelation 3:20 is often used as a call to nonbelievers, inviting them to faith, but in context it's an invitation to believers. Don't ignore the knocking at your door!

All three persons of the Trinity are represented in these letters. The *Son* is speaking to us, but each letter also includes the mandate to "hear what the *Spirit* says to the churches." And the *Father* is assumed present, as illustrated in verse 21. John wants us to remember the exquisite beauty and perfection of the Trinity who calls us to eternal community.

23. What reward does Jesus offer those who overcome their lukewarm tendencies (3:21)? We will explore this incredible invitation in detail in our next lesson on Revelation 21–22, the last two chapters in the Bible.

FINAL THOUGHTS

But the judgment of God is upon the Church as never before. If the Church of today does not recapture the sacrificial spirit of the early Church, it will lose its authentic ring, forfeit the loyalty of millions, and be dismissed as an irrelevant social club. . . . I am meeting young people every day whose disappointment with the Church has risen to outright disgust. Maybe again I have been too optimistic. Is organized religion too intricately bound to the status quo to save our nation and the world?
—Dr. Martin Luther King Jr., Letter from the Birmingham City Jail, April 16, 1963

24. If you did not answer the first question in the lesson, go back and consider your answer now.

25. Do you struggle with self-sufficiency? If so, can you discern why? What will it take for you to give up your need for control and finally depend on the Lord?

Yes, I do not like to ask for help.

Gradual commitment

26. Is the Holy Spirit convicting you that you are lukewarm in any area of your spiritual life? If so, what do you plan to do about it?

27. Evaluate your own life and the life of your worship community. If Jesus were writing a letter to you or to your community, what elements would he include?

DIGGING DEEPER

Write a letter to yourself and to your community as an exercise in understanding. Challenge yourself and your community to higher standards and greater rewards when Jesus returns.

DIGGING DEEPER

Look back over your lessons on the seven churches. Summarize the flaws that saddened the exalted Christ. Summarize the qualities he praises. From this analysis, describe the ideal church.

Our Eternal Home

Revelation 21–22

When Christians die, they go to heaven. But what will heaven be like? Is it endlessly floating around on clouds, playing harps, with little to think about or do? Conventional pictures look like that. The Bible shows us an entirely different picture, a far more interesting and realistic panorama, something to anticipate with wonder and excitement.

In this study, we skip chapters four through twenty, the account of God's final wrath upon the earth, not because these chapters are unimportant, but because, for believers, they are not the *most* important chapters. Go back and read them, and be grateful you won't be there. But in this study we are focusing on the sections that pertain more to our personal futures.

Throughout our journey in the seven letters, the exalted Christ gave us glimpses of eternity, but John ends the book with two chapters that tell us so much more. They don't tell us everything because our finite minds can't grasp it all, but we see enough to spur us on to live in hope and expectation.

This lesson covers Revelation 21–22. In these passages, scholars argue over what is literal and what is figurative, what is exactly the way it will be and what is a symbol of something impossible for us to fully comprehend. Let's not argue over these questions. Let's simply agree that these words are inspired by the Almighty God, that they are breathtaking and incredibly exciting. Let's agree that they give us hope, and they help us persevere as we attempt to live out the lessons we learned in the seven letters.

John's vision is full of dynamic images mixed together: a brilliant city, an elegant wedding, walls of jasper, giant pearl gates. Pictures of life abound: the book of life, the tree of life, pure life-giving water flowing from God's throne in waterfall cascades. All that is beautiful and blessed is there, twirling together in splendor and majesty, created as the place for us to worship God for eternity.

Walk with me through the city as we take in the highlights. Take in the sights and smells. Listen for the soothing sounds, and rejoice that you are the bride of the Lamb.

OPTIONAL

Memorize
Revelation 21:6–7
It is done. I am the Alpha and the Omega, the Beginning and the End. To the thirsty I will give water without cost from the spring of the water of life. Those who are victorious will inherit all this, and I will be their God and they will be my children.

I am overwhelmed as I write this lesson, inadequate to lead you through it. But God has provided these words, pictures, and prophecies to encourage us in this fallen world where we live, so I'll try. My fervent prayer is that you are overcome with hope and strength to live well until our new home is a reality. I can't wait to meet you there and hear your story as we worship, serve, and celebrate our God for eternity.   —Sue

 **Read Revelation 21–22.**

ALL THINGS NEW

1. Picture what John saw in 21:1–2. When John's vision comes to pass, how will life as we know it have changed? How final is this transformation? What are the four new names given to our new home?

2. What did God reveal to John about our eternal life in 21:3–4, 7? How do you feel as you read these amazing promises?

3. The sea was an instrument of God's wrath early in the earth's history (Genesis 6–9). Instead of the salty sea, what will God provide for his children in their new home (Revelation 21:6; 22:1)?

ETERNITY AS HUSBAND AND WIFE

4. One of the seven angels in Revelation whisks John off in another vision. What does the angel show John in 21:9? What does this suggest has occurred? See Revelation 19:6–9. What does this imply concerning our eternal state with God?

For your Maker is your husband—the LORD Almighty is his name . . .
—Isaiah 54:5

One time in my life when I fell deeply in love, the force of this passage struck me. No matter how much I might love, my love was only a shadow of Christ's love for us. Perhaps any symbol communicates only imperfectly the depth of Jesus' love for us, but our best approximations of unselfish love, such as a strong marriage, can provide us some beginning sense of it.
—Craig Keener
(*Revelation*, 509)

5. Next the angel shows us our new home (21:10). What details regarding our home's appearance does the angel supply (21:11–14)? What is significant about the two sets of names that are written on the gates and on the foundations?

The overall impression of the city as a gigantic brilliant jewel compared to Jasper, clear as crystal, indicates its great beauty. John was trying to describe what he saw and to relate it to what might be familiar to his readers. However, it is evident that his revelation transcends anything that can be experienced.
—John Walvoord
(*Bible Knowledge*, 985)

I love jewels—their color, their brilliance, the way they capture the facets of light and sparkle. I wonder if God created them to give us a tiny taste of the glorious future he has planned for us, his beloved. Imagine a whole city made of precious metals and stones—it takes my breath away and makes me ecstatic about our future together!   —Sue

6. When God created mankind, he placed us in a garden, but our future abode is a city. This megacity defies any place we have ever known. It is as tall as it is wide, probably square in shape. Generally, what is your impression of this massive city (21:15–21)?

CITY OF LIGHT

Why is there no temple in the new heavens and the new earth? Because in the Old Testament, the temple was the place where God dwelt. His Shekinah glory in the innermost part of the temple, the Holy of Holies, made the temple sacred. But now God physically resides with his people and thus there is no need for a temple ever again.

7. Three things will be missing from this city. What are they and why don't we need them (21:22–23)? What does the absence of celestial bodies imply about the new heavens, the atmosphere surrounding the new earth?

DIGGING DEEPER

Read and dissect Isaiah 60 to learn how God revealed the new heavens and the new earth to his early followers.

8. In 21:24, John says the nations will be included and "the kings of the earth will bring their splendor" into the city. Who do you think are *the kings of the earth*? What is John suggesting by this statement?

9. Why were city gates closed in the past? Why is there no need to ever shut the gates of this massive holy city (21:25)?

THE CENTER OF THE CITY

10. Describe what John saw in the middle of the great city (22:1–2). What do you think might be the significance of the water, trees, and fruit?

It's fascinating to connect the rewards Jesus promised those who are victorious in the seven letters we studied with different aspects of the new heavens and the new earth.

11. What will end and how will this change life as we know it (22:3a; Genesis 3:15–19)?

12. How has *the curse* affected you personally?

13. The relationship between men and women was severely impacted by the fall. The NET Bible translates Genesis 3:16b: "You will want to control your husband, but he will dominate you." Can you think of occasions when men and women attempt to compete and control one another? How will life be different without this aspect of the curse in effect?

14. What will people who loved and followed God be doing in this majestic city (22:3–5)? See also 2 Timothy 2:12a and Revelation 5:9–10.

15. Considering how God fashioned you with gifts, passions, and interests, how would you like to serve God for eternity? What do you think this might look like in the new heavens and new earth?

FINAL WORDS FROM JESUS TO JOHN

16. What does Jesus proclaim in Revelation 22:7, 12?

17. The last command in the Bible is found in 22:8–9. What happened and what is the command?

18. Jesus told John to write down and share what he has seen, heard, and learned with the seven churches, and ultimately us in 22:10. Why?

"I have come home at last! This is my real country! I belong here. This is the land I have been looking for all my life, though I never knew it till now. . . . Come further up, come further in!"
—Jewel (C. S. Lewis, *The Last Battle*)

19. In what sense is our time near, regardless of when we live on the earth? How much time do you think you have left in this life? How do you plan to spend it? Has your decision changed by studying Revelation? If so, how?

20. In 22:14, Jesus blesses those of us who have *washed our robes* with the right to live in the eternal city and enjoy eternal life with him. Have you washed your robes? If not, what is keeping you from entering into these marvelous blessings? Consider talking about your questions with a woman who loves and knows God.

The only thing which disqualifies a man from entering the presence of God is sin; the only thing which will qualify him to enter is to have his name written in the book of life of the slain Lamb. . . . Either he trusts in the crucified Christ for the forgiveness of his sins, or he is excluded from the Presence. *If you do not believe that I am he you will die in your sins* (John 8:24).
            —Michael Wilcock
                (*Message*, 211)

21. The Spirit and the bride make a final plea in 22:17. What is the plea and what is the free gift?

22. What are the warnings in verses 18–19? What do you think this means? How serious is God about the way his Word is handled?

23. Jesus makes us a promise in 22:20. What is his promise? How do you feel about this truth?

FINAL THOUGHTS

24. How has your study of the seven churches and the new heavens and the new earth affected your view of Jesus Christ?

25. How has this study impacted the way you think about your future? Are you expectant? Fearful? Oscillating? Can you determine why?

26. What have you learned from others in your group? Can you recall particular insights that encouraged or challenged you? Has anyone inspired you in your walk with Christ? If so, find an opportunity to tell them.

 What's Next? (*3:38 minutes*). Whatever you are facing or will face, good days are ahead!

27. As you prepare to make your home in the new heavens and the new earth, how can you continue in your efforts to persevere in what you have learned?

Works Cited

Caird, G. B. *The Revelation of St John the Divine*. London: A. and C. Black, 1966.

Fee, Gordon D. *Revelation*. New Covenant Commentary Series. Eugene, OR: Cascade Books, 2011.

Glasson, T. F. *The Revelation of John*. The Cambridge Bible Commentary on the New English Bible. Cambridge, England: Cambridge University Press, 1965.

Keener, Craig S. *Revelation*. The NIV Application Commentary. Grand Rapids: Zondervan, 2000.

Kent, Carol J. *Tame Your Fears: And Transform Them into Faith, Confidence, and Action*. Colorado Springs: NavPress, 1993.

Osborne, Grant R. *Revelation*. Baker Exegetical Commentary on the New Testament. Grand Rapids: Baker Academic, 2002.

Pentecost, Dwight. *Prophecy for Today: God's Purpose and Plan for Our Future*. Grand Rapids: Discovery House, 1989.

Walvoord, John F. *The Bible Knowledge Commentary: New Testament*. Ed. John F. Walvoord and Roy B. Zuck. Wheaton, IL: Victor Books, 1983.

Wilcock, Michael. *The Message of Revelation*. The Bible Speaks Today. Downers Grove, IL: InterVarsity Press, 1975.

About the Author

S ue Edwards is associate professor of Christian education (her special-ization is women's studies) at Dallas Theological Seminary where she has the opportunity to equip men and women for future ministry. She brings over thirty years of experience into the classroom as a Bible teacher, curriculum writer, and overseer of several megachurch women's ministries. As minister to women at Irving Bible Church and director of women's ministry at Prestonwood Baptist Church in Dallas, she has worked with women from all walks of life, ages, and stages. Her passion is to see modern and postmodern women connect, learn from one another, and bond around God's Word. Her Bible studies have ushered thousands of women all over the country and overseas into deeper Scripture study and community experiences.

With Kelley Mathews, Sue has coauthored *New Doors in Ministry to Women: A Fresh Model for Transforming Your Church, Campus, or Mission Field*; *Women's Retreats: A Creative Planning Guide*; and *Leading Women Who Wound: Strategies for an Effective Ministry*. Sue and Kelley joined with Henry Rogers to coauthor *Mixed Ministry: Working Together as Brothers and Sisters in an Oversexed Society*.

Sue has a doctor of ministry degree from Gordon-Conwell Theologi-cal Seminary in Boston and a master's in Bible from Dallas Theological Seminary. With Dr. Joye Baker, she oversees the Dallas Theological Sem-inary doctor of ministry degree in Christian education with a women-in-ministry emphasis.

Sue has been married to David for forty years. They have two married daughters, Heather and Rachel, and five grandchildren. David is a CAD applications engineer, a lay prison chaplain, and founder of their church's prison ministry.